ISBN: 1508489882
ISBN-13: 978-1508489887

for anna and grace

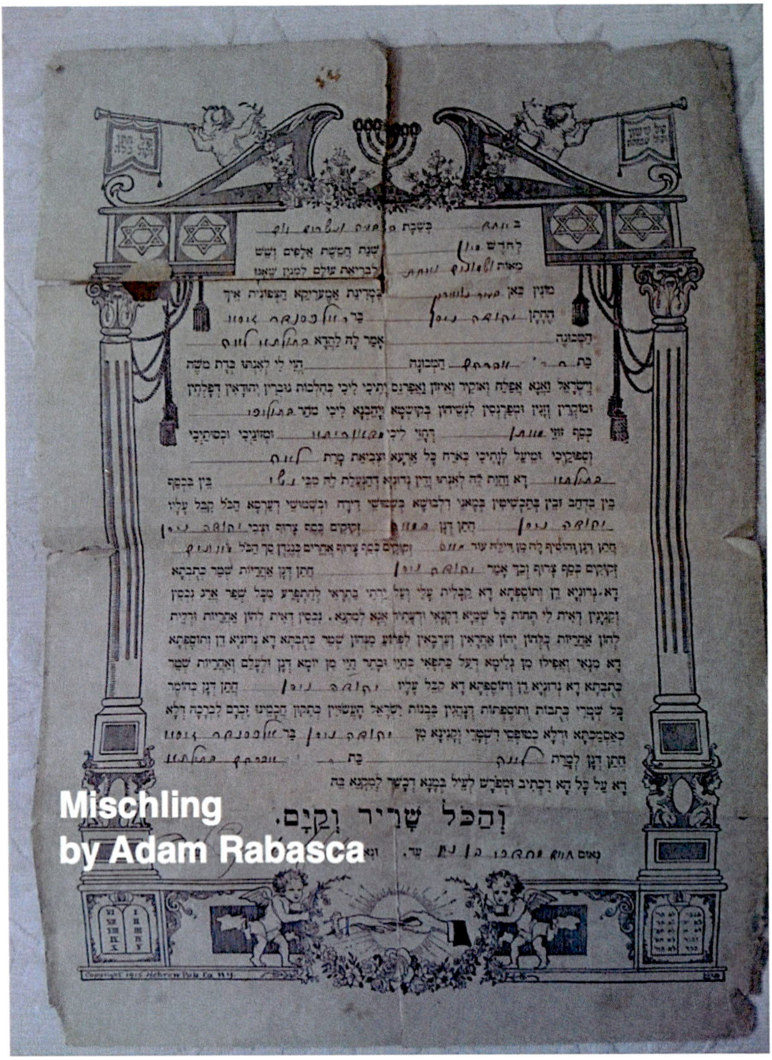

Mischling
by Adam Rabasca

in the space between birthdays

(1) The regulations in § I are also valid for Reich subjects of mixed Jewish blood [*Mischlinge*].

(2) An individual of mixed Jewish blood is one who is descended from one or two grandparents who were fully Jewish by race, insofar as he or she does not count as a Jew according to § 5, Paragraph 2. One grandparent shall be considered as full-blooded if he or she belonged to the Jewish religious community.

-II. First Regulation to the Reich Citizenship
Law of November 14, 1935

here,
the bright cosmic chasm
filtered beams -collectively spraying-
a pressured void,
expanding, charged

here,
cleaving two atmospheres
magnetic fields, their binding

here, time infused
in exhaustion
silence shuddering
frequent particles
withheld in
timelessness

here, i am here

i prefer order
definition

floods, frameless,

i cannot abide the plains
not even when
straight

the sea,
rhythmic
placid
firm

its rooted mists quell
little else than floodless
corners

order purging this relentless amalgam

whether it ebbs
or expires

seemly-

it is seemly

the quiet,

accessible space

inconspicuous
(non)compelling
contriving stillness
            festering negative plains
breeds lamenting spontaneity

an opaque space

a present space

a deliberate space

these indeterminate facts

a de-categorized fog

an avaricious hyperbole, an embellishment

this, untold time

        a past

        of ella
                her letters
                her silenced letters
                her disappearance
                her disappearing silenced letters
                her disappearing silence

        of *colombo*

records lifting
but for in book, penned by falsehood

this, reconstruction

        of indefinite endings
        while quarters end
        the fourth ending
                        her disappearing silence

        recalling the usurping whore
                beckoning her husband nearer

here, in decomposition

within dust from creaking bones
dust from skin

here,
        within mind, within night

he is here
not crying, nor i,

i am your grandfather,
i am here
if only briefly

beams croak and bend   in this cavern

you have to take care of
your parents, now

he is not crying

i,

i...can't do this

here is gone
he is gone

mischling

half-bred
children
adequately rid of condition
unlike their father
and the purged

purged the mongrel
the mongrel blood
mongrels only of two
kike veins
their unholy refuse
the mongrel horde
and its communism

no one will remember
no one will query the bygones
your mother's mother
descends into bygones

an ambivalence
of fact
of yes
descending with
bygones and
the blessed era of
death
and knowing the never

those, one fourth
those, half bred

those mongrel children

their mother remains
widowed
fatherless

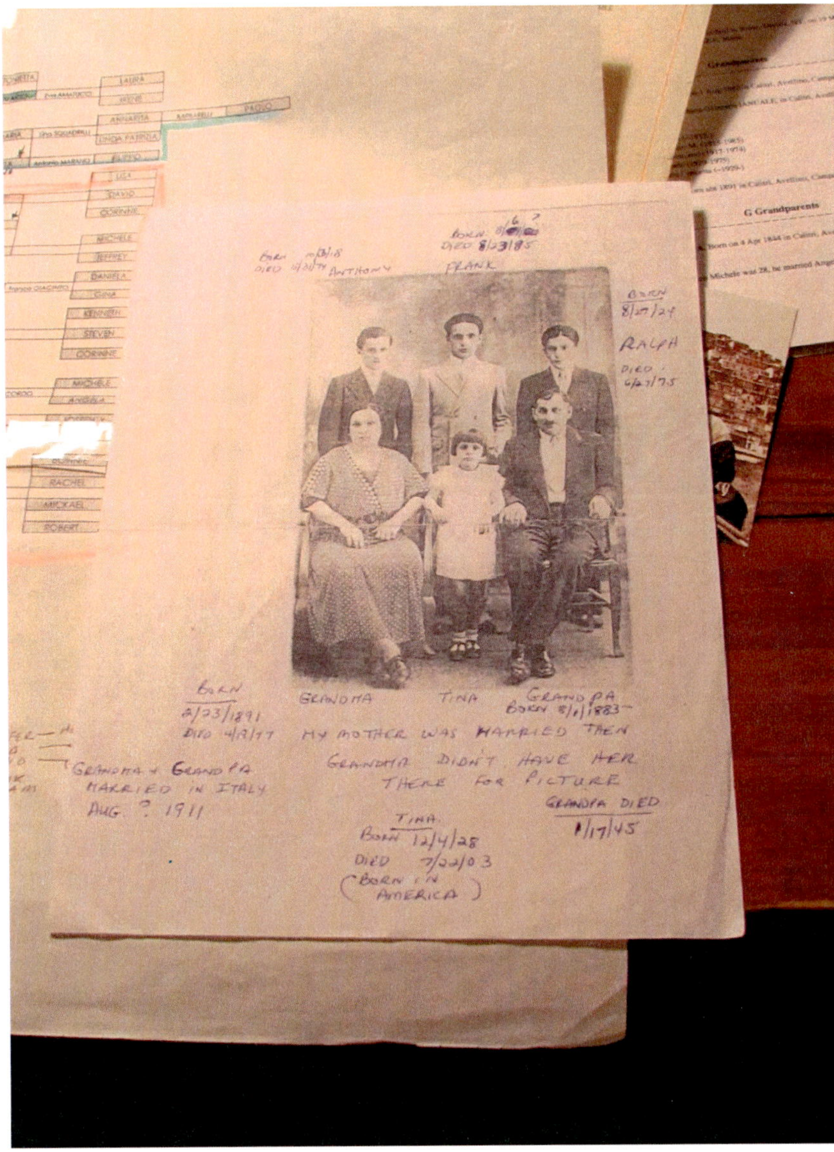
ANTHONY
DIED 8/23/85
FRANK
BORN 8/27/24
RALPH
DIED 6/27/75
BORN
2/23/1891
DIED 4/2/77
GRANDMA
TINA
GRANDPA
BORN 8/1/1883
MY MOTHER WAS MARRIED THEN
GRANDMA DIDN'T HAVE HER
THERE FOR PICTURE
GRANDMA + GRANDPA
MARRIED IN ITALY
AUG. ? 1911
GRANDPA DIED
1/17/45
TINA
BORN 12/4/28
DIED 7/22/03
(BORN IN
AMERICA)

june thirteenth nineteen twenty-seven

antonio

angelina, his older sister
frankie, his older brother
ralphie, his younger brother
tina...antoinetta, i think, was born here

colombo

genoa
colombo

these names
not unlike these names
the names of siblings
and villages

an elder sister
-angelina, perhaps-
unknown
(or unremembered)

absent
in the presence of
the boys
and tina

because she was ugly

the ugly should be
unaccounted for

in pictures

in record
repeating names
and surnames
and names of surnames
and surnames of their
surnames
the names of surnames
repeating repetition

gelo
ina
io
ela
gelo
ina
io
ela
gelo
ina
io
ela

the ginzos
without their papers

michele without his
papers
preceding children
without their papers

colombo
the depth beneath and above
cataclysmic hands holding insubstantial

evidence for thwarting worms
frenzied by feast

angelina,
the ugly, without her papers
outcropped, marginalized
by disavowal
be pretty

be seemly
beneath unibrows
and the greasy hairs
adorning lips and chests
and navels

gelo
ina
io
ela
gelo
ina
io
ela
gelo
ina
io
ela

be seemly

harbored
in summer's urban heat

humidity and stench
the three boys and tina unborn

gelo
ina
io
ela
gelo
ina
io
ela
gelo
ina
io
ela

each ginzo without
his papers or her
papers
disembarking for engulfment

this consuming amoeba
devouring ship and papers
its wake rushing to shore

chastising
memory, without its papers
and tangibles, without their papers
paperssssss
papersss
papers

gelo
ina
io
ela
gelo
ina
io
ela
gelo
ina
io
ela
gelo
ina
io
ela
gelo
ina
io
ela
gelo
ina
io
elagelo
ina
io
ela
gelo
ina
io
ela
gelo
ina
io
ela

calitri

calitri, east
seas sundering two families

each,   the wintering underbelly,
clutching
a trinket
a cloth
a hat

throwing to sea
waters festively greasing
a mountain
a village
a road

michele rabasca claiming a sign
emergent in white stone
-somewhat yellowed-
the photographic shadow diluting lens
within cropping
undiscovered until
two generations past

the boys and tina and the ugly

the sepia mob
enter this amoeba
vitantonio
growing a tentacle
inserting
into the amoeba's nucleus
a black fortress

diaspora
from calitri
forming barbs
        forming teeth
        forming teeth with barbs
        puncturing the hollows within cheeks
        while yellow and green oil drips from corners
        already callused by teeth and barbs

their masculine eyebrows
injected into another east
apart from origin east
columbo long departed
home's village
a city
        walled off by cold sight
        claustrophobic steam
        and sweaty odors saturating wool coats

by will or force
          -or forced will-
latin divergence splaying
          across field
          across soil
          and disdainful grievance
          -sewer rats teeming through manholes
                    breaching confines
                    and merging
as vitantonio
migrates eastward
closer to home

this ocean, black, forlorn, an electric barrier silent, without escort, his slumber vacillating between amoeba and origin, his blackness visible from space, swallowing memory, severing then, molecules thought dissipating within brine, within atmospheric distillation, vapors swiftly evanescing, escaping gravity and lifting towards heaven's deafness

letters' end
ending immediacy
of letters

send insulin

your father
half-brother, half-sister
someone

letters' end
soused in temperature

-escaping buckled light
the dysmorphic corpses-

send insulin soon

i told her,
no, mommy, don't go

the last one i write,
send insulin now

elizabeth
–perhaps elisheva–

- the alluring romance
of death and dying-

sent west
aunts and uncles
-are they even romanian?
an opportune construct?
an eager bastard?
the rest,

a nebula
though likely my own

memory loses active particles
though each molecule
exists as another's molecule
incestuously another's spoiled
molecule

now,
a newer matter
constructing a newer memento

each a convenient memento
until julius

i told her,
no, mommy, don't go

home,
ending letters

begetting speculation
we would have heard

something,
even something

particles amalgamize, distending themselves, and this, mischling, boiling off encrusted mucus, hammering at barnacles chewing into membranes, years of petrified brume, stalactites dripping into stalagmites, the two ultimately touching forcing into one another, a tree growth waxing more rapidly than branch, suffocating the latter, though the tedium of ghosts concludes defeat

papers

here,
galvanized tin
corroding liver spots
snug between sweaters and
otherwise unseasonable items

a social security card
a birth certificate
as brown at edges as her tan

a marriage license in yiddish
a marriage license in english

a leather pouch
crumbling biomatter
pleading for renewal

here,
elder hands
find them
gently on the bed
covered by a white throw

leather dusts the spread

his presence, absent
here,

where once we stood
uninvited
barefoot on the smooth plush rug

the canned leather
beyond that very wall
much to my oblivion

were alchemy the medium for reconstitution, perhaps a singular particle might elude fusion, absconding, two others, maybe three, preserving integrity, even if only momentarily longer, momentarily beyond constriction, sharing breath with those expiring –as a thief, breath might steal its nebula, handing into gravity's defense nothing,

said of the unsaid silenced

nothing may be said

not night, not whistles,
not deep bells,
or not breeze;

no night, for nazi lions, their howls and
sight boiling my skin, inexplicably

unsaid
nothing said, mischling,
ever

daughter,
daughters, both

chewing remains
weathered

some particles detached,
some molecules reacted,
volatile electrons discharged,
a fusion -or fission- of origin

falsehoods memorializing biologically,
remembering requiring alchemy

blood moon,
identical reddened orbs
blooming from heads, the same
risen unacquainted grandfathers

when either took air,
bled clean wounds,
ate meat

either unknown, unknowable
names,
though records must aid
acknowledgement
named historically,
historical by history
gelo
ina
io
ela
gelo
ina
io
ela
gelo
ina
io
ela

a blood moon's
inexistence
to them, nor those now,
an abstraction, conceptual, indefinite,
undefined,
and useless

here, mischling, consuming decay, ravishing humus, the composting irreverent magnetism a bloodied field, subtle dementia hosting steaming maggots aching in ecstasy, diminishing phantom corpses, a skeletal compote, primordial, perverse, the erasure of cleanliness, gray matter now degenerating, decomposing nutrients for feeding, an organic jelly remains dripping through this mischling's fist

s

for whom i am named

a musician,
smoothly fictitious

who returned in vaporous fog, speaking in chemicals only, in electric flows, soundwave particles congealing, balking fission, clotting bonds, known elements eradicated from earth, dissolved in exile, an unsatisfying explanation for gravity's bind, this shadowing title

no less, no more a name, but a name still, *his* name emerging from flesh

a flight from POGROM

-in speculative imagination- -in glamorous imagination-

the very mother who spawned him expelled him from home, whether by violence or intimidation, revoking citizenry through leonine ferocity

POGROM -another, perhaps- a separately probable incident, a culmination of nuisance, this S yields no response, no conclusion

this S a POGROM

to remain nameless, indeed, omissions
from this deep book's sullied pages
loosening fibers agreed upon in unison to
fuse the squandered fog, as damp breath
lays hold, constricting mercilessly before
releasing a final gasp, until cinching once
more the particle's abiding airway

in this space,
within raining haze

the field broke, divided

all substance smelted
into petrification
pulverized

such futile cycles

clarinets

sisyphus, my memory
memory, my stone
my stone porous
its nucleus sifting dust

dust, curdled marrow
stunned, disjoined
unglued (dis)continuum,
these plains
valent
or repulsive

this mindless field,
its atmospheric presence dissolving
radiation, ripples becoming
asymmetric

a solar flare melding
gentile and jew,
unbred for purity
unborn a mischling

those european children

those of children,
those of europe
those

of stippled descent
of grayness from one hand
of questioned archives,
whether POGROM or flight
whether hunger or disdain
perhaps as contemptuous
(or regretful)
as just

gelo
ina
io
ela
gelo
ina
io
ela
gelo
ina
io
ela

those, plunging into the great, great amoeba
in systematic, distant arrangements

those no longer generationally clustered
those without their papers,
    their papers without papers

here, swallowed,
    here, absorbed

those european children,
        now,
        matter of the great, great amoeba

s

blue-gray or burgundy, undoubtedly, undoubtedly roundhead brass pins fastening fabric, a dissolving plush

the curvature of mahogany legs, their oiled grain, darkened in sensual, routed grooves of a child's finger repeatedly tracing the depression, languishing indoors from cold spells and tired humidity

re-upholstered, newly a focal piece controlling windows boasting white trim dividing panes, less than a room from the *mezuzah*, which on dimming evenings affixed its dulled bronze nostalgically to long island, south of jerusalem

this S, where he collapsed ghosting his
imprint, molding a missing being, all but
the pipe incensing the ceiling

no one ever occupies the chair,
except my father with the weekend news
and his coffee

ceramic mugs without cigarettes nor dogs

away, away the camouflaged stain, six
pipes and their faint aroma, their brass
feet and dirty curves, imprisoning hirschl
and bendheim, the corn-cob, the
briarwood, the ivory hand growing from
its black shaft, knotted, cloaked, the
geometric kaywoodie, the kentucky
burley, bristled metal, filters, a wheatie,
and hickory enveloped sweepstakes
tickets, sailing abroad from doncaster

and the butterflies -oh, the butterflies-
nailed to the pale, pale walls, deeply blue
with eyes instead of wings, so delicate
beneath their glass, their black
monstrous bodies bordered by golden
wood

the pastel room designed only for peace;
how quietly the upright thumped broken

notes
-the length of the cream carpet-
untuned, cracked notes
two keys unresponsively flat

the S corpse draping his legs across the embroidered bench, florally blued, teeming with notes his daughter refused

wooden, maple
or alder
perhaps oak

inquisitive S collecting time,
raising the flattened keys manually hammering for sound,

an unsettling, ricocheting tone
resonating disquieting success

no music of POGROM

no sound of exodus
no rhythm of march
no exodus of audis and
northbound *garmentos* donning crisp mustaches and greasy skin, generously opening their wallets during weekends to petite wives and bowl-cut children, wearing skin-tight jeans hugging muscular stout thighs

this S, pleasantly curled in remodeled upholstery
asleep, within cubicles

designed by heavenly composition's new pattern,
intersecting squares, light blue, peach, stitched with white cordoning

it is he who created me
i am his creation -i am his S-

in association
with one jew
transferred into birth, transferring jews to diffusion, spreading jews to the animal,
the animal within amoeba,
birthing another jew
moments before quietus

S

bodily disposal collecting detritus,
inserting into child, blood-borne chronicles

chromosomes of mechanical waves, the

deep one crashing blatantly on tears and drying sands, whipped at uselessly by neon beach towels, two decades worth of grime and overgrowth

S

mischling
S

stomping upon the graves of beth moses, unruly junipers clawing at brazen, screaming children, kangaroos trampling grass on the southern side of cedars, beyond which lie further corpses, corpses awaiting visitors, corpses feasting on corpses, corpses wishing the burial of corpses, the feasting of corpses, the feasting of S, of mischling corpses, of pedigreed corpses, of corpses no one wishes to ever be rebirthed, of corpses fornicating with soil, of corpses restrained by earth and organic composite

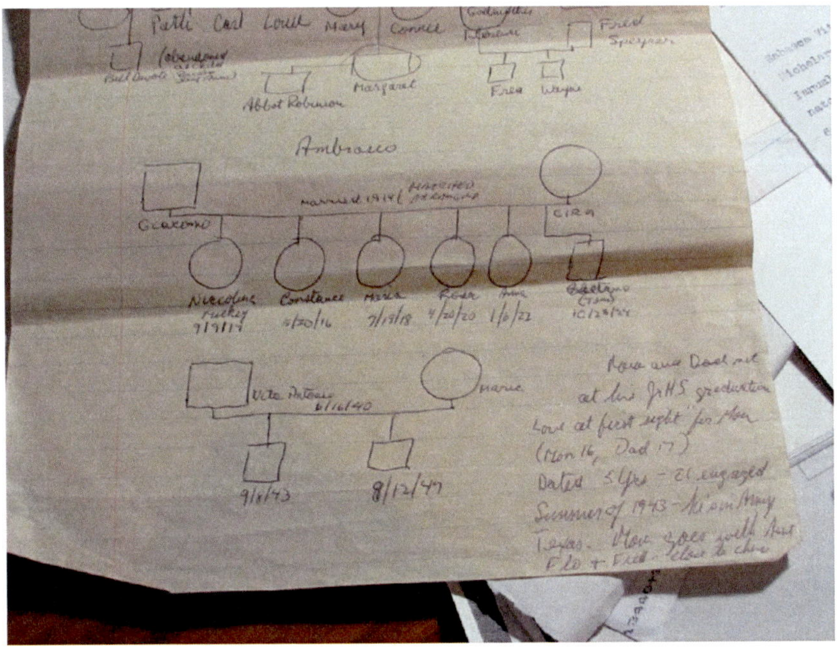

Patti
Carl
Louie
Mary
Connie
Fred
Margaret
Abbot Robinson
Fred
Wayne
Ambrosio
Cira
Constance
5/30/16
7/19/18
Rosa
4/20/20
Ann
1/6/22
Vito Antonio
6/16/40
Marie
9/8/43
8/12/47
Love at first sight
Summer of 1943
Texas

outward,
ivy pockets, bricks of the fifties, a manicured hilltop cut by blacktop -the unlikely fact- perhaps, flatstones or flagstones forming walls, flagstones forming flatstones, forming drainage pipes of indeterminate origins (in which we hid eggs - the eggs over which i pouted when it rained) and metal downspouts releasing waste, a bared tree for ascension -a single adjacent neighbor of whom no recollection exists, another's presence beyond limbs and fences, eyes of watchers and automobiles, the corridor strangled by ivy leaving pockets and snaking away from the sun

raised upward,
porcelain hummels -collectors' items for sexagenrians older than today- andes candies, the idiot box, miniatures of owls upon owls, the green of carpet- perhaps shag, the dimming sheers, the floral couch, a shadowing mirror, a milk glass lamp, a thin refrigerated bowl too tiny for small hands, untouched rooms, unlit rooms, unmade rooms, unopened rooms, unlivened rooms, down a lightless corridor

beneath,
green plastic army figurines, aging lincoln logs aged from her children, toy indians kept in corners, dark and quiet imbibing vision in flourescence through betrothed halls and shabby couches likely now the property of dollar movie theaters and used bookstores

northward,
a framed man accompanied the second exodus from a home she never loved and forever missed in a state apart from

gelo
ina
io
ela
gelo
ina
io
ela
gelo
ina
io
ela
gelo
ina
io
ela
gelo
ina
io
ela

creased pictures introducing strangers, to my father, these papered without papers, their sweat cascading image to skin, drenching mine, gluttonous traces dusting my oiled fingertips, then brushed off with disposable rags, the gloss yielding to pressure, invading inward so as to erase such distinguishing features, the brow priestly, protected, his force inherent in expression, uniformed guards thrusting rapiers beleaguer in uncertain safety, the brow (again) obvious, downward from steps, a fortress background drawing observation to his pale, pale robe, their surrounding darkness in defiance of besieging monsters and monsters within, he delivers the shroud of turin rabasca, his name is ours, fleeing campania for avellino, a mission of little import but for symbolic defeat, while eastward, a quiet devil defiled unforeseen convergences, though merciless history surrendered our monk to this elemental plain, shreds of his fabric, his brow, his brow, his brow, abandoned to soil mother and son(s)

his memory, merely
protein constructs,
proteins building neurons,
proteins firing into synaptic voids

his construction,
remembered partially in dementia,
damaged fibers rendered useless
a third party shaping,
molding falsehoods
molding casts
molding casts fit for impure protein constructs
                                        impure neurons
                                        impure synaptic voids

neutron particles collapse, collide
cooly within brain tissue
                -with brain meat-
the more she remembers,
the less true in retelling,
as proteins escape
through membranes
born for failure
for weeping over expression

a graying son
                -the one who looks like sean connery-
the faucet releasing an emergence of protons
during which he will look up, only outside

at his unnatural garden
years before now,
her tiny voice

he was changing a tire

debatingly, impatient

it was a massive
coronary, mom,
he was eating lunch

her dainty hands retrieve ideas
-the owls and porcelain hummels survived,
    and the idiot box
    and a glass cart-
coffee cans glued with floral paper
crafts with seniors
pride lost in routine,
lost on youth

an elderly freezer
meat tins four months old
a care package,
morsels for the long drive home
    -she could not understand how
        i could eat them without sauce,
            and cold-

return the garden pond behind
a stone stool on which three sat
-it didn't matter that she wasn't italian
or that she was looking elsewhere-

grandmother,
eyes downcast,
contemplating
grains and crystals composing rock
as old as she feels

still expiring through glass
the garden pond collecting proteins
no longer embraces purpose
dna chains diverge,
severing mother and son,
exiling both to polar cells
fleshy orbs pinching dead matter
as she upsets him with complaints
of the queen, exasperated

the mindless hubris,
clean in composition
yields lesser flaws, porosity
expanding,
contracting solid meat
the meat rare
discolored and shrinking
reaching backwards
ever further backwards
the unattainable food
on which now feeds

little original dna remains,
little face, little awareness,
little ego,
within super ego,
their weak design, inorganic,
season's tyrannized governance
breeding vitriol in its loins
steaming, wet
warming the itch
before inserting dominance

a demon of breath
surging within channels,
coiled and beastly
and poised for slaughter

of record

salvatore antonio rabasca- his first heart attack -mild- a warning, the second -more severe, third- fifty-four -january after trying to change a tire in a snowstorm -never fully recovered -may- died at the lunch table with a massive coronary while grandma was at work

-he was the first to die of his generation-

children of two
jewish grandparents = *mischlinge (first degree)* = kike
rabasca (father)

children of one
jewish grandparent = *mischlinge (second degree)* = children of kike
rabasca (daughters)

the satan is the jew the satan is the
jew the satan is the jew the satan is
the jew the satan is the jew the satan
is the jew the satan is the jew the
satan is the jew the satan is the jew
the satan is the jew the satan is the
jew the satan is the jew the satan is
the jew the satan is the jew the satan
is the jew the satan is the jew the
satan is the jew the satan is the jew
the satan is the jew the satan is the
jew the satan is the jew the satan is
the jew the satan is the jew the satan
is the jew the satan is the jew the
satan is the jew the satan is the jew
the satan is the jew the satan is the
jew the satan is the jew the satan is
the jew the satan is the jew the satan
is the jew the satan is the jew the
satan is the jew the satan is the jew
the satan is the jew the satan is the

the satan
is the jew
the satan is the jew

the satan is the jew

the satan is the jew

yid hymie canadian goose abe christ
killer hebe (or heeb) kike (or kyke) beanie
oven-dweller cliptip hooknose lampshade
shylock snipcock fagin penny chaser
campers (dual reference) nazi candle

second degree sleep

the fields calmed but for expanding silence
sleep, as perhaps one had been
the trite equalizer
a figment ghostly spraying sedatives
over frenzy

was ella *that* mother,
    the infant clutching her neck
    her bones intact when found
    beneath depths of soil
    decomposing mass corpses
    their guilty blood satiating
    earth's thirst,
    the child surviving execution but not the dark,
    the taste of dirt,
    while clawing into mother

was ella mother to a small girl
    hung by meathooks,
    bleeding five jews
    now kosher by predatory hands,
    carved flesh reading the mock blessing,
    drained in a slaughterhouse,
    dripping into troughs,
    fresh wine for blessing

was ella shuffled through streets
    spat upon

rogue bullets piercing neighbors
the perpetrators neighbors
the police neighbors
the neighbors neighbors funneling
into courtyards surrounded by neighbors
neighbors pulling breath
from newly formed corpses
the new wine rinsing grime
from the neighbors boots

this silence, second degree,
this past

sisyphus' S

i have never been a protein nor a neuron
unless in reflective alternatives, a parallel
plain, a distant plain, free form and blindly
sullen

several universes beyond ours, its
expanding limits, its limitations, though a
replica (replicas) exists, perhaps ease
might belong to another:

another rabasca,
another romania
another russia
another calitri
another mischling

symmetrical repetition, the alternate
needed no insulin, kept no ocean, no
colombo, no longer gravity's S

annals, though, exist in symmetry,
whereby memory remains, dementia
preserved, the bloated S, the punctured
S, sisyphus' S

saving but a single protein, dementia lessened, metabolic decay slowed, a letter held, the distillation of particles delayed, primordially black, the froth steaming into gaping nostrils arguing for air

then, perhaps,
sisyphus ascends once less

No. 1436965

THE UNITED STATES OF AMERICA

CERTIFICATE OF NATURALIZATION

Petition, Volume F- 482 Number 116011

Description of holder: Age 32 years; height 5 feet 4 inches; color

dark ; color of eyes brown color of hair brown

marks none

Name, age and place of residence of wife none (Single)

Names, ages and places of residence of minor children none.

ORIGINAL

Julius Schwartz

STATE OF NEW YORK

COUNTY OF NEW YORK

S.S.

Be it remembered that Julius Schwartz

mischling root

opaquely a brown panelled
unfocused wall, complexion pale,
head tilted left with an aging
gristly pompadour, lips pursed in
song, microphone held to chin, a
crisp suit, i cannot imagine his
voice, nor his languish

overlooking central park, painted
winter, sleds tossing children in
red jackets, gray trees scarring
apartments, i see him, listless,
my father carried him to bed,
understanding breath would exit,
skin would sag into his bed,
yellowed

my only knowledge, though he
took breath after my birth, i've
been told much but i don't see
him

only the mischling S

american-born russian jew
clarinetist, the instrument resides
in vermont, his voice dispersed
over solar flats, though unlikely
rattling in an asymmetrical
universe, even with this slight
formation, an anomaly brushed
from irritating microfilaments

i long for that reed, for breath to
extract from mental detritus his
intonation, his timbre, its
crescendos, its irregular staccato
syncopating nightfall before
ocean's swell floods imagination,
drowning particle and protein,
stamping ions, their charged
medulla eating itself

a cheap plastic light plugged into the papered wall, singing melancholy hebrew

a fleeting spiral reformation though compositionally altered, another rapacious clock sweeps proteins from thought, penurious, destitute, nursing its own cavities

while we fast, the orange plastic eradiates glowing sorrow, dust floating exposed, covering our empty guts in shallow mist

his replacement, always familiar, recalled vagueness of erroneously white suits, both now expired, flesh exhausted and peeling, sagging from compressed bones,

my grandfather
a jew

un-

an emaciated proton colliding
with another beginning anew,

the gray S, expunged mischling
colombo destined elsewhere
POGROM never fabricated

of those un-mixed
we ignore
though not favored
when convenience requests

it lays quietly speculating
the counterpart motive
so extroverted
in voice
in sight
ignore the taste for organic
matter repulses all too easily

fields

an alternate field
swirling within its self-imposed boundaries,
the likelihood of occurrence increased
exponentially by particle volume

were it POGROM,
validity might be accessible,
-but since when was validity prerequisite-

beth moses might miss
the absence of his bones,
might question his approach,
though later, if ever

were the alternate real,
that sepia island
might keep safe annals of
our four branches, though maybe
in reconstituted matter
the reconstitution unbelievable
fertilizing an alternate field
the alternate gnashing roots
of blistering roots
before fixing
the toxic nitrogen

such chronicles might
preserve sequence,
the two never orphaned,

the progression and dissidence
preventable,

otiose regret ground to paste,
molded into a freshened scroll
before the pulp smothered itself
across our eyes
in secrecy

the same boat, the same locale
readily, their will to emigrate
a negative blank neglected,
unfilled
unfillable
incomplete

spaces exist between annals, hideous between the glutton amoeba and nest over saline, brine itself diffuse with nostalgic attraction, linear or planar, whether in flux, whether static, the spaces bubble, consume, thinning membranes, oily surfaces to which no protein may adhere, amoral, the plains dilated in all directions with impunity marauding serfs

such as we are,
such scavenging crows

fettered to that decrepit scroll,
the disintegrating leather pouch,

his cherrywood pipe holder,
her empty, papered cans,

his asthmatic camera,
its shutter wheezing under
duress of use,
her promise ring stolen

his discordant piano
partitioned and shelled,
upholstery incinerated,
ablaze in elemental
bliss

a euphoric escape,
vestiges splintering, shards slicing into
white, white carpet,
compacted while her husband prepared
me for death

ridgefield

here,
where a secretary once stood,
the room bare
but for a brown wicker chest,
a glass nightstand hosting elephants
with upturned trunks
-said to be of good luck-
a stained dresser,
its brass handles tarnished from
thirty-year-old oil

images cached within glass doors,
the few recalled resurrect
little of that generation
though paintings remain

replicas -except in winter views
from a hospital window
before dying-

one of fruit, eggplant,
green from darkness
despondent

another of a marionette
or a boy,
the title escapes,
the legs disproportionate

and physically impossible,
an error in proxy

held in hand, the same
to a pipe, a corn cob

a brush stroked
the one asleep, a girl in dress
shoulders bared of lace
sorrow in the dining room,
a gray cat,
or sand

each placed away
given away
away northward
away in between walls and dressers

each memento cast aside
to youth with
no room for storage
no room for a shrine
no room for exhibition

the regal design, golden
for nothing

the look of the poor

if i were young again
greasy locks stabbing my eyes
the look of poverty, of non-wealth
        of homelessness
        of nomads
        the glamorous bohemia

absorption in all non-necessity,
all that is social, the brashness of heat
and fervor

one might
                with strength
                        or will
                        or defiance

        or with desire enough

gather each particle
        each droplet fired among synapses
                those reddening fissures

the walls, the potential to withstand
the brutality of unending

and synthesize the
future of electricity and protein construction
into a convincing argument
allows the poor
a moment of vision
a momentary understanding
of the maelstrom
to be cleaved

s ep ara ted

from heart
feeling
and the assurance

of knowing

in her coffin, body confined to stifled cellular atrophy, her carcass emerging from melanomas, fading liver spots, painted brows, an untouched casket, weeping fathers, one unconsoled by offspring so close, the legacy of piecemeal assemblies, merging into one another, releasing structure, fornicating with the earth and leaching into her soil

here

nearer,
this origin of departure only steps
behind pistols,
swallowing bullets slower than the speed
at which they
exit my throat

apathy spiders
through membranes
suturing wounds with venom
and fibrous silk
far too porous for clotting
the bleeding
(onto fabled cobblestones)

here,
a nucleolus, an atrophied screen,

stealing
terrorizing
another's collections
molesting their innards
and laying naked
the remains for putrefaction

-insufficient guesswork indeed,

even with hoarded scrolls,
shredded papyrus transparent
from prints and prints
of prints
carelessly folded and tucked in-

such are
abandoned in this pith

still time,
still, unquestioningly
time

a moment breaths,
exists,
remains present,
and persists within itself

the grains of a moment,
perhaps when letters ceased
yet living,
pixelated, composite
ploughing green landscapes
in place of maggots

preservation of
this moment
halted,
though it rots its own season
a pebble hidden
within her tiny grip

it exists now,
it exists
yesterday

perhaps particles of that
moment will converge,
forging elements unseen

amidst spraying radiation,

the heated fog,
scorching
this charged field

his talon, extends haplessly from midnight, reaching the hull via tributary tentacles, gliding over depths familiar only to those who attempted yesterday in their own reaches through parallel continuums, disturbing orderly leaf piles, autumn punctured, all that is visible rippled through this single portal oh, the glory

from *shtetls*
gunned down in breezy fields

tall blades tickling racing elbows
an iron guard greasing their axles,
(with lacerated thighs or calves)
sickening the axis

fact exists separately
at least until the amoeba engulfs
the fortunate,
their journey only ending
one nightmare before
fleas ultimately
finish the job

what mind
whether impregnated or creative,
manufactures such mechanical acts
to drain victims
and incorporate their bodies
into machine
into raped abscesses
discharging their bloody ejaculate

of record

julius smoked luckies
sometimes they called him julie

of a single photograph, he and elizabeth,
stillness between, outside home

-everyone wore black pants
and short sleeve button-downs-

there were no luckies in the picture

of record

julius was in the first war, nineteen
twenty-one, by her account, two
daughters named roselyn and francis

elizabeth's mother died when she was a
baby and so was sent to new jersey,
cared for by her aunt and uncle

they spoke only english
not romanian

of record

samuel stanley kaplan's father, born in
the blizzard of eighteen eighty-nine,
smoked chesterfields
three brothers, though

he drove a truck and
almost made it to one hundred

one died at normandy
his mother, anna, russian born

lieber
liebowitz, lieberman

it escapes me

of record

the jewish catskills, nighttime visits, singing to welcome the new night, nineteen thirty-nine bears significance, though it was england in forty-two or forty-three

the commanding officer was fond of him, kept him in the band, a mention of dancing and returning on saturday nights by train, she was not in london

of record

her second husband, laurence, was in the ski patrol, switzerland, germany, austria, he was a color reviewer for the daily news, cartoons and comics, the camera was his

his sons doug and jonathan -the latter died in a mid-air collision over san diego- doug, the same birthday as the mischling

now,
one resides with beth moses, the other cremated, though some say "disturbing," feeding a potted plant outside the kitchen window

she talks to him everyday

florida

of his known to me,
the fluorescent hats,
the demo racquets and disintegrating grips

eccentric devices
-a taser, a pocket knife, gold watches,
point-and-shoot cameras, a jar of
change, a flashlight-
disorganizing the bottom drawer of
his ivory bedstand

the gasping aperture
needing repair,

swallowing lost shots

cigars, fat and savory
as a child on his lap,
sucking smoke in deeply
expelling it across a chasm
towards alternate plains
in which he still may exist
his pancreas intact

here enters my chemical presence

overlapping occurrences draw
time into focus from
stark metallic vistas

what alloys dwell
do so with disinterest
the passivity of youth
coinciding with neglect
and blueing forget

singular echos
laying dismissively within
contextually mapped scapes within
transparent grids
leveling within simple millimeters
within a spectral ocean's flux

here inlay sweltering heat
humid stench
palms refusing sway
hairspray attracting mosquitoes
in tight white shorts and tube socks

sweat glistening our brows
seizing vital proteins

their voices drowning
into gray-green clay

the sound of repetition,
the graphite stroke swung
evening sets
over tape and netting
over nails and grit
and careful measurements

a pink solar glimmer
tickling space

such massive grains
spattering image

both boys at play,
he taught the little one

and when finally,
after an empty span
they touched clay together
once more and
for a final time

an unfortunate of
lost timing
followed him
to death

STATE OF NEW YORK, COUNTY OF NEW YORK, ss.:

I, ARCHIBALD R. WATSON, County Clerk and Clerk of the Supreme Court, New York County, do hereby certify that I have compared the attached marriage certificate and affidavit with the original thereof filed in my office and that same is a correct transcript of the original and of the whole thereof. IN WITNESS WHEREOF I have hereunto set my hand and affixed my official seal.

NOT VALID UNLESS RAISED SEAL IS AFFIXED

JUL 5 1957

[signature]

COUNTY CLERK AND CLERK OF THE SUPREME COURT, NEW YORK COUNTY.

No. [illegible]

STATE OF NEW YORK

Affidavit for License to Marry

INDEXED

Date of Marriage: June 1921
Church:
Location:
Clergyman: Shapiro, Riv. St.

STATE OF NEW YORK
County of New York, City of New York } ss.:

Julius Schwartz

and Elizabeth Davis

applicants for a license for marriage, being severally sworn, depose and say, that to the best of their knowledge and belief the following statements respectively signed by them is true, and that no legal impediment exists as to the right of the applicants to enter into the marriage state.

FROM THE GROOM	FROM THE BRIDE
Full name: Julius Schwartz	Full name: Elizabeth Davis
Color: White	Color: White
Place of residence: [illegible] st. New York City, N.Y.	Place of residence: [illegible] ave. [illegible] N.J.
Age: 22 [illegible] 1921	Age: 22
Occupation: [illegible]	Occupation: Dressmaker
Place of birth: [illegible]	Place of birth: [illegible], Romania
Name of father: [illegible] Schwartz	Name of father: [illegible] Davis
Country of birth: Romania	Country of birth: [illegible] Romania
Maiden name of mother: Rosie [illegible]	Maiden name of mother: [illegible]
Country of birth: [illegible] Romania	Country of birth: [illegible] Romania
Number of marriage: First	Number of marriage: First
I have not to my knowledge been infected with any venereal disease, or if I have been so infected within five years I have had a laboratory test within that period which shows that I am now free from infection from any such disease. No	I have not to my knowledge been infected with any venereal disease, or if I have been so infected within five years I have had a laboratory test within that period which shows that I am now free from infection from any such disease. No
Former wife or wives living or dead: None	Former husband or husbands living or dead: None
Is applicant a divorced person: No	Is applicant a divorced person: No
If so, when and where divorce or divorces were granted:	If so, when and where divorce or divorces were granted:

Julius Schwartz
GROOM

Elizabeth Davis
BRIDE

Subscribed and sworn to before me this 15th day of June 1921

[signature]
Clerk

[illegible] STUB 5527

JUL 5 1957

elephants with trunks upturned

this,

a regeneration of protein,
though composition be reconfigured
solids conjoined by fibrous scars
seams pasted organically
though hastily,
far more hastily than the organ's intent

but a long breath,
inhaled from the mother -the earliest-
exhaling once on the conception of
the second-degree
lest we forget those rooted
to the grand amoeba

the fullness of breath,
untidy, rich, bodily breath

though temporal fixation
never rebirthed in
such composition

fleeting as memory
fleeting as greenery (the annuals)
fleeting as the taste of
such bloodied atmospheres

they are mischlinge
and from which, the meandering splits
down encrusted mounds
of raw, raw keratin

they are mischlinge
grown from spit
and yet still external

mischling

bleed the jew
diminishing blood
of its fullness

first degree,
my half body
half-body
half *bris*
half kike

second degree,
the mischling's progeny
the expression equalling adequate

children
whose higher degree depletes
further the jew that no longer exists

diffusing matter, the organic diaspora
the grinding bone
against another's sour wounds

returning bucharest's slaughter, the kosher feasting,
returning such minute distinguishing
returning POGROMPOGROMPOGROM
returning:

gelo
ina
io
ela
gelo
ina
io
ela
gelo
ina
io
ela

returning:
POGROM ravaged supple muscle
POGROM reigned
until trains asphyxiated passage

corpses held corpse in urine, in waste
in vomit
in the pervasive stench of
muddied skin

my corpse, in stone
instead, the ghost molesting
so perversely its glistening pus

i was not on the transnistrian train,
converging westward with or without family
destined plains,
fertilizing earth,

jew marrow,
cracked from new carcasses,
spilling into
european soil
as *colombo* escapes

odessa bled, iaşi bled
bucharest bled

spewing teeth at children,
faces unsystematically slumping,

selected not randomly
not in elitism
rather
by history

[secular, non-secular =
such formulations mattered little]

final
POGROM

the nonrelatives, though nameless,

all but ella
the one
querying insulin
the one
elizabeth could
not see

american letters burned
or saturated,

into meal by sputum,
drained from dead mouths,

moistened ground untraversable,
the feasted slain bodies

draining into rising yeast

our own blistered by wind,
spraying platelets,
miniature nodules lifting skyward
mingling into fog,

the reddened haze
inhaled by other bodies,
before their own enter mist
and fornicate molecule with
molecule
the bloodied mist fornicating
with alternate plains
with

as the wops fucked
their unseemly cousins
as the unwanted bled into earth
into each other's mouths
into each other's cavities
into each other's pores

until squeezed from eye ducts
until seeping infection amputated
the groping tentacle
until foreskins swallowed
and
bathed in the other half's sweat, fecal bed

their tongues lacerated

eyes punctured and
shaved
throats pierced
bile pouring from
wounds

flooding into sores
on their palettes
their splitting lips forced

open, their bleeding gums
screaming and
screaming and
screaming and
screaming
an d scr ea m ing a nd s
cre a m i n
gand scre am ing
a n dsc re a m i
ng
a n
d s c re a m
i n g a nd
s c r e
a m i
n g s
r e a
m i n g
s re a i

n g s e
a m in g
s a m
i n
g s
a m i
n g

s m
in g
s i
n
g s n
g
s
n

s
s
s
s
ss
sss
ss
s
s
s

s

until all suddenly halted

erased, uprooted
and branded,

mischling.

thanks to b. shimoda, p. cordelli, h. mitchell, m. gauthier, and my wife, elizabeth

quotes and correspondences from m. rabasca and r. falk appear throughout

documents and objects pictured within were provided by r. falk and t. rabasca

a quote from i. antonescu ("the satan is the jew") appears and is documented in sources too numerous to cite

i know so little of all that is true or real.

19619386R00060

Made in the USA
San Bernardino, CA
06 March 2015